Christian Poems for Toddlers

by
Mildred Morningstar

updated by
Marilyn Morningstar

Illustrated by Nadene Esterhuizen

Morningstar Media
Tucson, AZ 85739
Copyright © 2024 All rights reserved. Printed in U.S.A.

This book belongs to:

_____

My mother helps me every day,

When I dress and when I play;

Then she whispers in my ear,

"<u>Mother loves you, Dana dear.</u>"*

*Whisper in child's ear.

Jesus loves you more than mother,

More than father, sister, brother;

Jesus listens when you call.

<u>Jesus loves you most of all.</u>*

*Whisper in child's ear.

"We love because He first loved us." 1 John 4:19

I'm ready for breakfast; I'm up in my chair,

And I'm hungry too, for the food that is there,

But I'll fold my hands; my head I will bow,

And shut my eyes tight.

Look I'll show you how.

I thank you, dear Jesus, for milk in this cup,

And now for my fruit juice-I'll drink it all up.

I thank You for toast and for cereal too.

I'll make it "all gone;" just watch while I do.

"We love because He first loved us." 1 John 4:19

I like to sing; I like to play.

I like to go outdoors each day;

And in the swing I have such fun.

My brother's kind to everyone.

But Jesus up in heaven

Has loved me even more.

It says so in the Bible,

That's what God wrote it for.

"We love because He first loved us." 1 John 4:19

I have a nice big sister;

She shows me all her toys,

And pictures too, of Jesus,

Who loves the girls and boys.

He loved the little children,

And took them on His knee;

And now He's up in heaven,

Yet He loves even me.

"We love because He first loved us." 1 John 4:19

Dirty hands, oh, dirty hands,

I don't want two dirty hands;

I will wash them nice and bright,

Scrub them clean with all my might.

Dirty heart, oh, dirty heart,

I can't wash a dirty heart;

I'll let Jesus wash away

The naughty things I do and say.

"We love because He first loved us." 1 John 4:19

The nails hurt His hands,

And the nails hurt His feet,

And the thorns stuck clear down in His head.

He was thinking of me;

He was thinking of you,

And He died, but He rose from the dead.

The Lord Jesus knew

Of the bad things we do,

And He wanted to take them away:

He was punished for me;

He was punished for you.

I will thank Him

He loved me that day.

"We love because He first loved us." 1 John 4:19

We're going bye-bye today.

Knock, knock, knock at the door;

We've come to stay for a little while;

We'd like to visit and play.

Jesus is at the door;

Don't make the dear Saviour wait.

Answer the door as He knocks today-

Tomorrow may be too late.

"We love because He first loved us." 1 John 4:19

My daddy is the nicest man;

I watch for him each night.

I sit right by the window;

My face is clean and bright.

He kisses me and squeezes me;

And he throws me in the air.

Then he tells me that the Saviour

Loves children everywhere.

"We love because He first loved us." 1 John 4:19

The Bible is God's Word;

We read it every day;

And then all together

We kneel down to pray.

My heart's door was opened;

And Jesus came in.

The Saviour is willing

To save you from sin.

"We love because He first loved us." 1 John 4:19

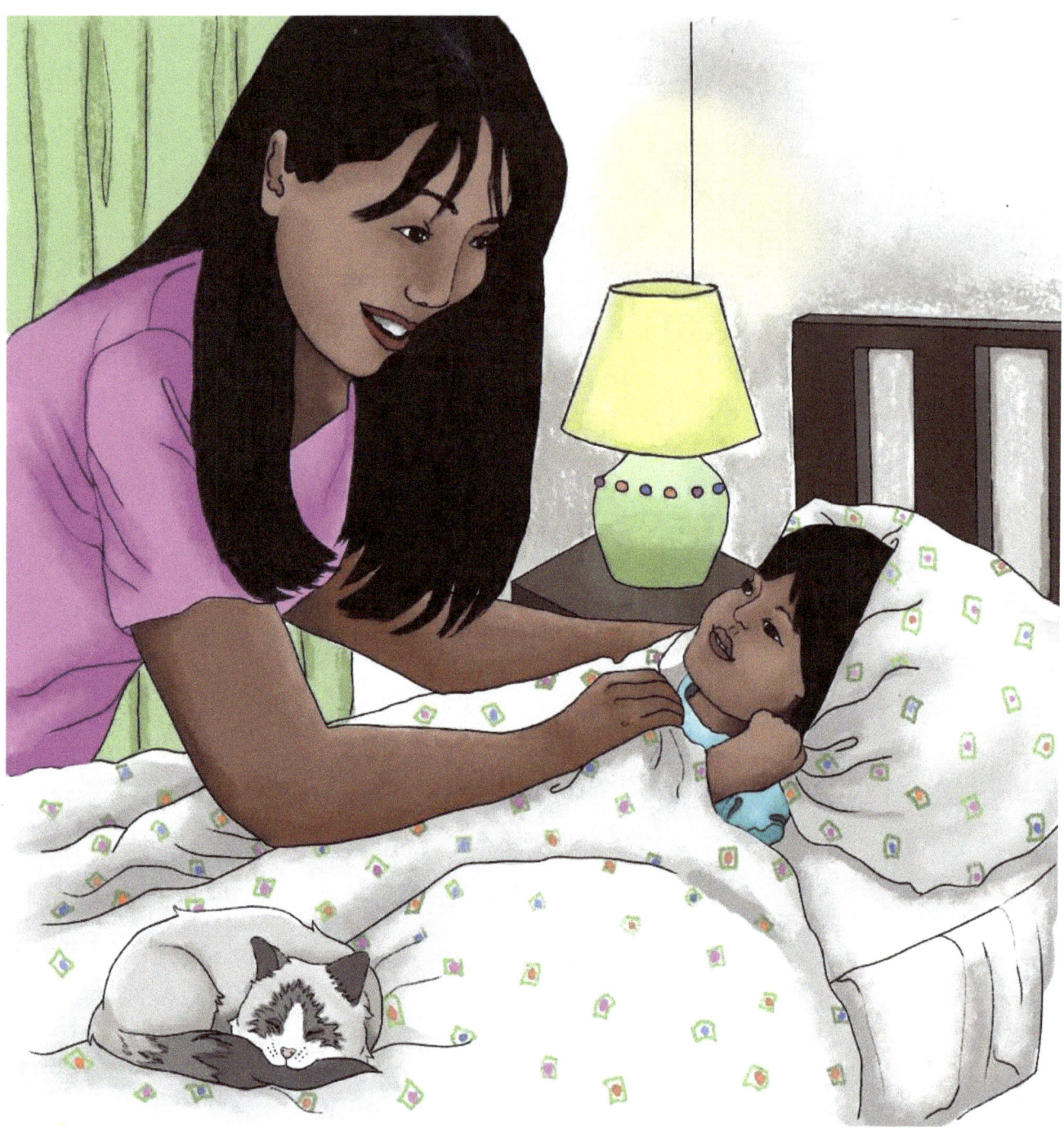

Nighty night, yes nighty night;

Up come the covers,

Out goes the light.

Mommy dear will put a kiss

On each rosy cheek like this.*

*Kiss child on each cheek.

Nighty night, yes, nighty night;

Jesus is with you.

Close your eyes tight.

He will keep you in His sight,

Safe until the morning light.

"We love because He first loved us." 1 John 4:19

For the Parents

I hope you enjoyed reading this book to your child. My mother wrote these poems in 1947! My mom was a wonderful Christian woman. She was a Kindergarten and Fifth Grade teacher; but her first love was writing for and about children. I wanted to have this book updated and republished to honor her love for children and God. Both my mother and I strongly believe that it is never too early to present the Gospel to small children.

Here are some verses from the Legacy Standard Bible that pertain to raising children in the word of God:

"Train up a child according to his way; even when he is old he will not depart from it."

Proverbs 22:6

"Fathers, do not provoke your children to anger, but bring them up in the discipline and instruction of the Lord."

Ephesians 6:4

"The father of the righteous will greatly rejoice; and he who begets a wise son will be glad in him."

Proverbs 23:24

About the Author

Mildred Morningstar has authored several books and has written articles for various Christian magazines. She graduated from Denver Bible Institute and Wheaton College.

Her books include *Reaching Children, Teaching Johnny to Give, Africa Comes Alive, Japan Comes Alive* and *The Amazon Comes Alive* (for children and teachers) and *Danger at the Sheep Ranch*. She has had articles published in "Moody Monthly," "His," "Today's Child," "Young Ambassador," "Success," and others.

Marilyn Morningstar is Mildred's daughter. She graduated from Moody Bible Institute and the University of Houston. She lives in Tucson, Arizona and attends Lifepoint Church (Catalina). She also volunteers in the stamp ministry of Global Recordings Network.

www.ingramcontent.com/pod-product-compliance
Lightning Source LLC
Chambersburg PA
CBHW060411010526
44107CB00006B/648